What's in this book

This book belongs to

_____

中秋节 Mid-Autumn Festival

学习内容 Contents

沟通 Communication

称呼家庭成员
Address extended family members

背景介绍：
中秋节，外婆在给浩浩和玲玲讲嫦娥奔月的故事。

浩浩外婆

生词 New words

★	外公	mother's father
★	外婆	mother's mother
★	来	to come
★	休息	to rest
★	老	old
★	哭	to cry
★	笑	to laugh
	舅舅	mother's brother
	阿姨	mother's sister
	叔叔	father's younger brother
	姑姑	father's sister
	电话	telephone
	喂	hello (when answering the phone)

句式 Sentence patterns

舅舅和阿姨也来了。
My mother's brother and sister also came.

叔叔和姑姑没来。
My father's younger brother and sister did not come.

跨学科学习 Project

认识全球受欢迎的节日
Learn about the popular festivals around the world

文化 Cultures

庆祝中秋节的方式
Mid-Autumn Festival celebrations

Get ready

参考答案：
1 I see a full moon about once a month./Only sometimes because I do not pay much attention to it.
2 Yes, I have./No, I have not.
3 People enjoy the full moon and eat moon cakes on that day./I do not know.

1 How often do you see a full moon?

2 Have you heard of the Mid-Autumn Festival?

3 Do you know what people do at the Mid-Autumn Festival?

读一读 Read

故事大意：
中秋节，浩浩一家和外公外婆等人
在花园里赏月、吃月饼、点灯笼，
一起欢度节日。

妈妈的哥哥或者弟弟
我们都叫"舅舅"。

wài gōng
外公

wài pó
外婆

jiù jiu
舅舅

ā yí
阿姨

妈妈的姐姐或者妹妹
我们都叫"阿姨"。

"来"是指动作向自己（说话人）靠近
的这一过程。"来"的反义词是"去"。

lái
来

参考问题和答案：
1　What festival is it? (It is the Mid-Autumn Festival.)
2　Who are the elders sitting at the table? (They are Hao Hao's grandma and grandpa on the mother's side.)
3　Who are the younger persons sitting at the table? (They are Hao Hao's aunt and uncle on the mother's side.)

今年中秋节，外公、外婆在我家。
舅舅和阿姨也来了。

...火节，人们通常会和家人一
...赏月、吃月饼，孩子还特别
...欢玩灯笼。更多的文化介绍
...看本书第18页。

我们在花园里吃月饼和水果。天上
的月亮圆圆的。

参考问题和答案：
1. What is Hao Hao pointing at? (He is pointing at the moon in the sky.)
2. How does the moon look? (It looks round and bright. It is a full moon.)
3. What are Ling Ling and Dad doing? (They are hanging lanterns onto a tree.)

爸爸的弟弟我们都叫"叔叔"，而爸爸的哥哥我们都叫"伯伯"。

shū shu
叔叔

爸爸的姐姐或者妹妹我们都叫"姑姑"。

gū gu
姑姑

爷爷、奶奶、叔叔、姑姑没来，他们去中国旅行了。

参考问题和答案：

1 Who are the people taking a picture together? (They are Hao Hao's grandparents, aunt and uncle on the father's side.)

2 Where are they? (They are on the Great Wall of China.)

喂，……

向人打招呼或与人通电话时，我们用叹词"喂"。如：喂，请问您是哪位？

diàn huà
电话

参考问题和答案：
What are Hao Hao and Dad doing? Why? (They are making a telephone call to Grandpa. Because he is in China and not with Hao Hao and Dad.)

他们的中秋节怎么样呢？我和爸爸给他们打电话："喂，……"

7

xiū xi

休息

lǎo

老

九点半，外公、外婆回卧室了，因为老人要早点休息。

参考问题和答案：

1 How do Grandma and Grandpa look? What do they need? (They look tired and they need to rest.)

2 Do Grandma and Grandpa look old to you? (Yes, they do./No, I don't think so.)

kū

哭

"哭"和"笑"是一对反义词。

xiào

笑

大家看着我和姐姐的灯笼，说："哭和笑，都好看！"

参考问题和答案：

1 Look at the lanterns the children are playing with. What is the design? (It is a design of a puppy face on the lanterns.)

2 What is different about the two lanterns? (Hao Hao's lantern is a crying face and Ling Ling's lantern is a laughing face.)

Let's think

1 Recall the story. Find and circle the mistakes in the pictures.

故事里是外婆，这是奶奶。

故事里是满月，这是弯月。

故事里是爷爷，这是外公。

故事里是智能手机，这里不是。

2 Role-play as the people in the pictures with your friend and say.

让学生理解并巩固各亲属之间的关系图表。在说话过程中，鼓励学生尽量用中文表达。

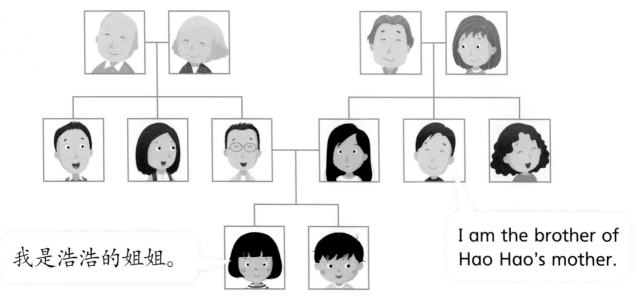

我是浩浩的姐姐。

I am the brother of Hao Hao's mother.

New words

1 Learn the new words.

延伸活动：
老师先让学生复习图中的亲属称谓及关系，然后两人一组，互相说一说自己有哪些亲属，以及他们与自己的关系。参考句式 "我没有……" "我有……他/她是我……的……"

2 Listen to your teacher and point to the correct words above.

第一题录音稿：
1 星期六，浩浩和外婆去了动物
2 她是个可爱的女孩，最喜欢笑
3 昨天，浩浩给叔叔打了电话。

 03 **1** Listen and circle the correct person in the pictures.

 04 **2** Look at the pictures. Listen to the story a

1 浩浩和谁去了动物园？

2 她最喜欢做什么？

3 浩浩给谁打电话？

玲玲，你怎么哭了？

我来了。我们一起做。

你看，玲玲笑了。

第二题参考问题和答案：

1 What is Ling Ling making? Do you like it? (Ling Ling is making a lantern. Yes, it is cute.)
2 Do you enjoy living or spending time together with your grandparents? (Yes, I love talking and doing things together with them./Yes, but they live in a different city so I only visit them in the summer.)

延伸活动：
学生可更换其他亲属角色后再进行对话练习，对话内容可以参考本题也可以自由发挥。

外婆，你来看看，我不会做这个。

你外公要多休息，他有点老了。

外公、外婆，谢谢你们！

3 **Write the letters. Role-play with your friend.**

a 休息 b 外公 c 来

喂，外婆你好。

喂，玲玲吗？

是的，外婆。明天你 __c__ 我家吗？

我明天去。

__b__ 呢？

他不去，他在家 __a__ 。

Task

Ask your friend to role-play as your grandparent. Make a phone call to invite them and other relatives to a family gathering.

提醒学生对话时需涉及题目中列出的要点，并可介绍一些打电话的礼貌用语："喂，您好，我是……""请问您是……吗？""再见。"

Things you
need to think about

星期几？

几点？

在哪里？

多少人来？

什么人来？

做什么活动？

Game

老师鼓励学生尽可能多地说出题中的亲属关系。
参考句式"……是……的……"

Colour the female family members red and the male family members blue. Then say who they are to your friend.

妈妈是阿姨的姐姐。

爸爸是叔叔的哥哥。

Chant

Listen and say.

延伸活动：
学生三人一组，分角色说唱歌曲。

喂喂喂，喂喂喂，
请问你是谁？

舅舅好、阿姨好，
我是浩浩。

外公、外婆在家吗？
外公、外婆休息了。

再见舅舅，再见阿姨。
再见浩浩，再见浩浩。

生活用语 Daily expressions

HAPPY HOLIDAYS

节日快乐！

Happy holidays!

TAKE A REST

休息休息。

Take a rest.

写一写 Write

1 Trace and write the characters.

提醒学生"哭"字不能漏掉一点"泪珠";"笑"字中的"夭"上面是撇不是横。

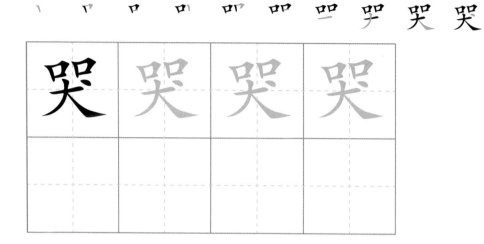

丶 丨 丨 口 口 四 四 哭 哭

哭 哭 哭 哭

丿 𠂆 𠂇 𠂉 𣥂 𣥂 𣥂 竺 竿 笑

笑 笑 笑 笑

2 Write and say.

他 哭 了。他 很 小。

她的脸圆圆的，她喜欢 笑。

16

提醒学生同一颜色的空位表示需写同一汉字，每种颜色只配对某一个字。
学生做完题目后，仔细阅读该段落加深理解。

3 Fill in the blanks with the correct words. Colour the balloons using the same colours.

粉色
因为

蓝色
生日

黄色
笑

昨天是我的 生日 ，外公外婆来我家了。我们唱 生日 歌，吃 生日 蛋糕。

因为 我大了一岁，我很高兴，大家也很高兴，我们都 笑 了。

拼音输入法 Pinyin input

One of the phonetic-based input methods is Pinyin input. When typing a character, first type the Pinyin, and then the number for the character you need.

Circle the correct numbers to type 'good morning'.

提醒学生在输入所打汉字的拼音后，会出现同音字与相同声韵母却不同声调的字，要注意选择要打的目标字。

zao
①早 2 造 3 遭 4 枣 5 燥 6 灶 7 糟 8 凿 9 躁 ◀ ▶

shang
①上 2 商 3 尚 4 伤 5 赏 6 裳 7 觞 8 殇 9 熵 ◀ ▶

hao
①好 2 号 3 浩 4 豪 5 郝 6 耗 7 昊 8 镐 9 蚝 ◀ ▶

多元学习 Connections

老师可简单介绍中秋节：中秋节是华人四大节日之一（农历新年、清明节、端午节和中秋节）这一天月亮满月，象征团圆。且中秋节正值秋季，人们同时会欢庆丰收。关于中秋节，古代中国还有嫦娥奔月的传说（可参见本系列的"中国文化入门"书第11页）。

Have you heard of the Mid-Autumn Festival? Learn about its traditions.

The Mid-Autumn Festival falls on the fifteenth day of the eighth month in the lunar calendar, in September or October in the Gregorian calendar.

Family and friends gather together to celebrate the unions and give thanks for the harvest.

The main traditions of the festival include eating mooncakes and lighting lanterns.

Project

老师可简单介绍下面四个节日：
圣诞节，12月25日。庆祝耶稣的诞辰。
新年，1月1日。庆祝新一年的到来。
排灯节，又称万灯节，每年10月或11月中举行。庆祝善行战胜邪恶、光明击退黑暗。
斋戒月，回历的第九个月。伊斯兰教徒在日出之后禁食，学习古兰经，日落之后可恢复正常生活。

1 Learn about some popular festivals in the world.

Christmas

We celebrate the birth of Jesus Christ.

New Year's Eve

People all over the world welcome the new year with fireworks.

Diwali

We worship the Hindu goddess of prosperity during this festival of lights.

Ramadan

For a month, we fast from sunrise to sunset to celebrate this Muslim festival.

2 Do some research on other festivals. Tell your friend about them.

鼓励学生带节日相关图片与大家分享，也可穿该节日的服饰回学校。

我喜欢……
它在……日。
那天我……

我喜欢中国新年，因为有很多糖果。

19

温习 Checkpoint

老师可先介绍：中秋节夜晚，人们会做灯笼，点灯笼，赏花灯以衬托月色，同时增添节日气氛。然后让学生完成灯笼上的题目，看谁又快又正确，最后给完成的灯笼涂上自己喜欢的颜色。

1 Complete the tasks on the lanterns and colour them.

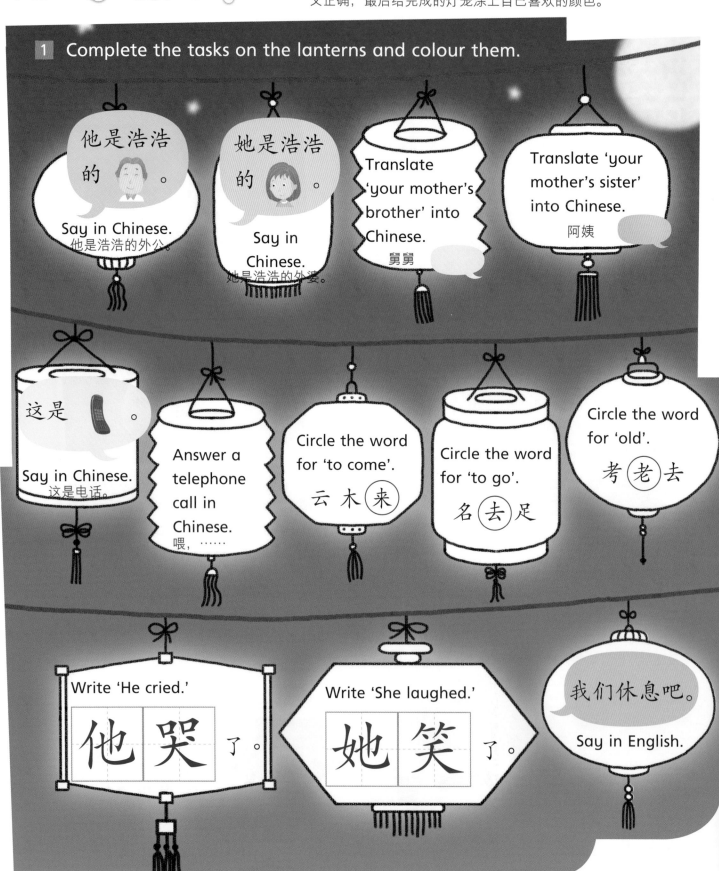

评核方法：

学生两人一组，互相考察评价表内单词和句子的听说读写。交际沟通部分由老师朗读要求，
学生再互相对话。如果达到了某项技能要求，则用色笔将星星或小辣椒涂色。

2 Work with your friend. Colour the stars and the chillies.

Words	说	读	写
外公	☆	☆	🌶
外婆	☆	☆	🌶
来	☆	☆	🌶
休息	☆	☆	🌶
老	☆	☆	🌶
哭	☆	☆	☆
笑	☆	☆	☆
舅舅	☆	🌶	🌶
阿姨	☆	🌶	🌶

Words and sentences	说	读	写
叔叔	☆	🌶	🌶
姑姑	☆	🌶	🌶
电话	☆	🌶	🌶
喂	☆	🌶	🌶
舅舅和阿姨也来了。	☆	🌶	🌶
叔叔和姑姑没来。	☆	🌶	🌶

Address extended family members	☆

3 What does your teacher say?

评核建议：

根据学生课堂表现，分别给予"太棒了！
(Excellent!)"、"不错！(Good!)"或"继续努力！
(Work harder!)"的评价，再让学生圈出上方对
应的表情，以记录自己的学习情况。

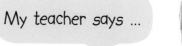

My teacher says ...

分享 Sharing

Words I remember

外公	wài gōng	mother's father
外婆	wài pó	mother's mother
来	lái	to come
休息	xiū xi	to rest
老	lǎo	old
哭	kū	to cry
笑	xiào	to laugh
舅舅	jiù jiu	mother's brother
阿姨	ā yí	mother's sister
叔叔	shū shu	father's younger brothe
姑姑	gū gu	father's sister
电话	diàn huà	telephone
喂	wèi	hello (when answering the phone)

延伸活动：

1 学生用手遮盖英文，读中文单词，并思考单词意思；

2 学生用手遮盖中文单词，看着英文说出对应的中文单词；

3 学生两人一组，尽量运用中文单词分角色复述故事。

Other words

中秋节	zhōng qiū jié	Mid-Autumn Festival
月饼	yuè bǐng	moon cake
天上	tiān shàng	sky
月亮	yuè liang	moon
旅行	lǚ xíng	to travel
打	dǎ	to dial
老人	lǎo rén	old people
要	yào	to need
点	diǎn	a little
大人	dà rén	adult
灯笼	dēng long	lantern

OXFORD
UNIVERSITY PRESS

Oxford University Press is a department of the University of Oxford.
It furthers the University's objective of excellence in research, scholarship,
and education by publishing worldwide. Oxford is a registered trade mark of
Oxford University Press in the UK and in certain other countries

Published in Hong Kong by
Oxford University Press (China) Limited
39th Floor, One Kowloon, 1 Wang Yuen Street, Kowloon Bay,
Hong Kong

© Oxford University Press (China) Limited 2017

The moral rights of the author have been asserted

First Edition published in 2017

Illustrated by Anne Lee, KK Ng, KY Chan and Wildman

Photographs for reproduction permitted by Dreamstime.com

China National Publications Import & Export (Group) Corporation is an authorized distributor of
Oxford Elementary Chinese.

Please contact content@cnpiec.com.cn or 86-10-65856782

ISBN: 978019-942995-0

10 9 8 7 6 5 4 3 2

Teacher's Edition
ISBN: 978-0-19-082260-6

10 9 8 7 6 5 4 3 2